LASSIE! GET HELP!

LASSIE! GET HELP!

CARTOONS BY DANNY SHANAHAN

Pantheon Books New York

FOR JANET AND RENNY

Library of Congress Cataloging-in-Publication Data

Shanahan, Danny.
Lassie! get help! : cartoons / Danny Shanahan.
p.   cm.
ISBN 0-679-73017-6
1. American wit and humor, Pictorial.   I. Title.
NC1429.S49A4   1990
741.5'973—dc20   90-52532

Book Design by Anne Scatto

Manufactured in the United States of America

First Edition

"It's cryin' time again, folks."

"Say, buddy, what time is it?"

PONY ESPRESSO

"I pinched a nerve just 'bob-bob-bobbin' along'"

As his head cleared and his eyes began to focus, he realized that it wasn't his only Sheila, it wasn't Sheila at all. It was a hologram of Ernest Borgnine fly-fishing the Saw Kill River, and a damned life-like hologram at that!

Shanahan

"Karl and I have decided to do the nursery
in twigs and bits of string."

"Can I call you back, R.B.? I've got a situation here."

CHICKEN À LA KING

"Someone's been sleeping in my bed, too,
and there she is on Screen Nine!"

YO! EMMETT KELLY RAPS!
(WITH RINGMASTER FLASH)

"Police, ma'am."

"Simon *says* interact!"

KONG FOR A DAY

"Please let me through, gentlemen. I'm a dental hygienist."

PUSS IN FACTORY SECONDS

THE ALL-MUSE TEAM

How they stack up defensively...

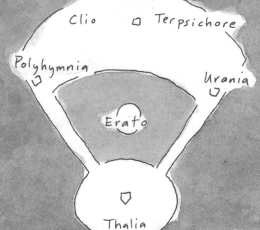

Calliope

Euterpe

Melpomene

Clio   □ Terpsichore

Polyhymnia
□

Urania
□

Erato

Thalia

Shanahan

Not an easy out in the lineup!

	Pos.	Name	Avg.
1.	2B	Terpsichore	.310
2.	CF	Calliope	.323
3.	C	Thalia	.298
4.	DH	Heracles	.440
5.	LF	Euterpe	.303
6.	1B	Urania	.317
7.	3B	Polyhymnia	.265
8.	RF	Melpomene	.301
9.	SS	Clio	.272

And on the mound...

	W-L	E.R.A.
Erato	11-0	1.05

Erato, daughter of Zeus, is a left-hander with a sneaky fastball, a withering overhand curve, and a screwball she'll throw to right-handed batters to keep them honest.

36

"Any fan mail for me today?"

41

42

THE FAB FOURSOME

"No wonder you can't hear the ocean.
You're listening to a croissant!"

"Who's Slingin' Sammy Baugh, Grandpa?"

"The brown eggs match your eyes, ma'am."

"You've got to understand, Mr. Duncan, that your
son Colin's arrowhead collection is of
major interest to my people."

"Polly's damn head is stuck!"

HIAWATHA ON HIS JET-SKI,
(ON THE SHINING BIG-SEA-WATER)

THE CHIPPEWA AWAITING THEIR TURN,
(ON THE SHORES OF GITCHE GUMEE)

Shanahan

"You may already be a mere footnote."

TALENT, PLUCK, OR PLAIN DUMB LUCK?

WHISTLER'S MOTHER AT SHARKEY'S

THE VILLAGE ID

"Read 'em and wet!"

"Lick the damned thing!"

The brooding monoliths of Chocolate Easter Bunny Island stand as mute testimony to an ancient civilization, a people long gone. They say nothing, yet they speak volumes. They say it with their enigmatic majesty; they say it with chocolate.

Shanahan

"How's about a hot slice for a harbinger of spring?"

THE KING OF COUNTRY MUSIC

PIERRE DE BUZANCAIS (French, 1885 – 1970)

Mon television, mon remote du television, mon guide du television, et mon snacks du television (1961)

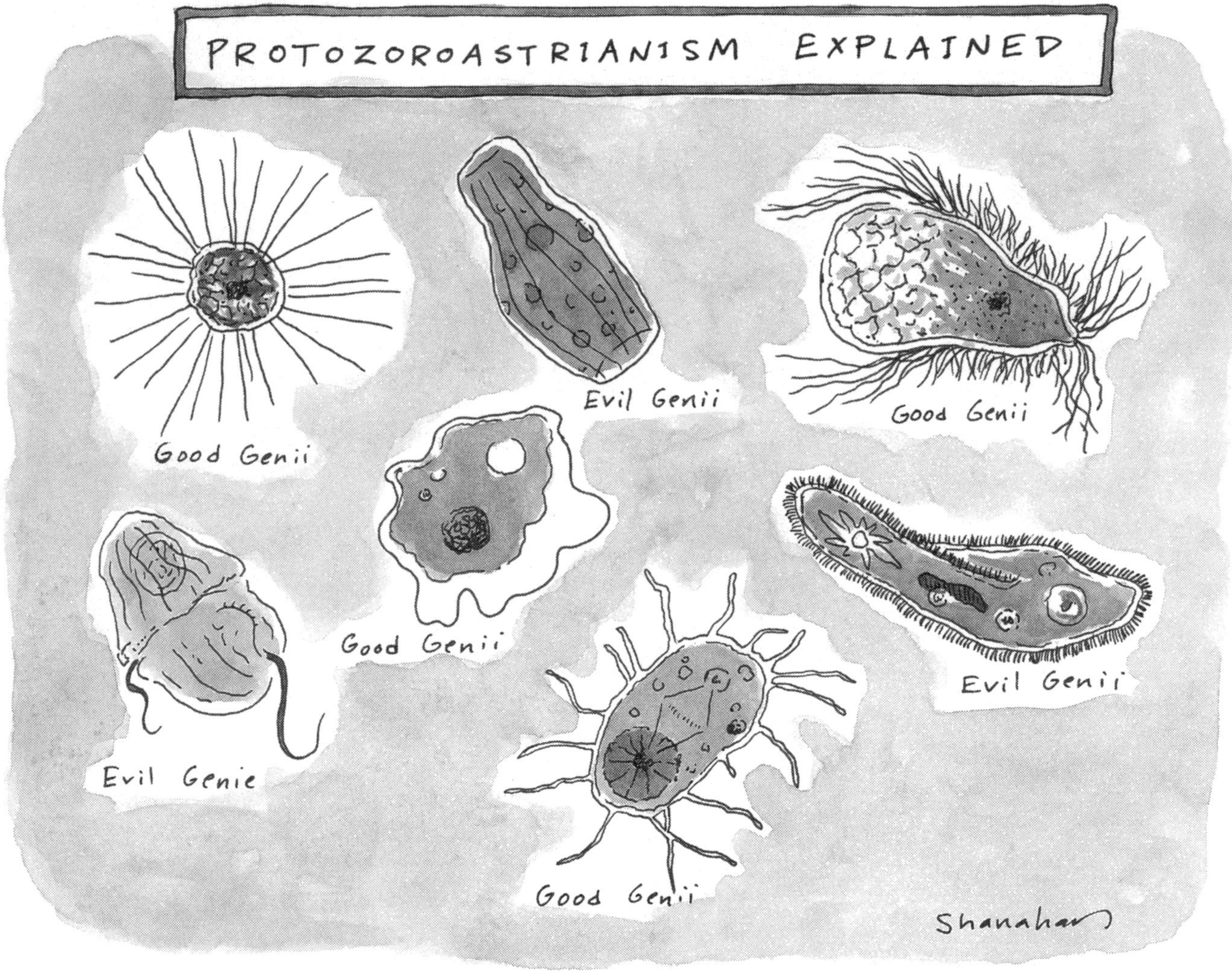

PROTOZOROASTRIANISM EXPLAINED

Good Genii

Evil Genii

Good Genii

Evil Genie

Good Genii

Good Genii

Evil Genii

Shanahan

"Productivity is way up, but there's been
an unfortunate increase in job-related injuries!"

THE HEART IS A LONELY HUNTER

"The macaroons are off!"

"And when my journey's over and my body's old and bent,
    There's one place only that I'll want to be,
    Take me back to Banbridge Head, and the Bay of Cluckluman
    There to watch the playful chickens of the sea, sea, sea,
    The fine and glorious chickens of the sea!"

"The kohlrabi is crisp, fresh, and delicious.
In all else lies madness."

"Uh-oh! I just felt something go crunch.
I hope it wasn't the cappuccino machine!"

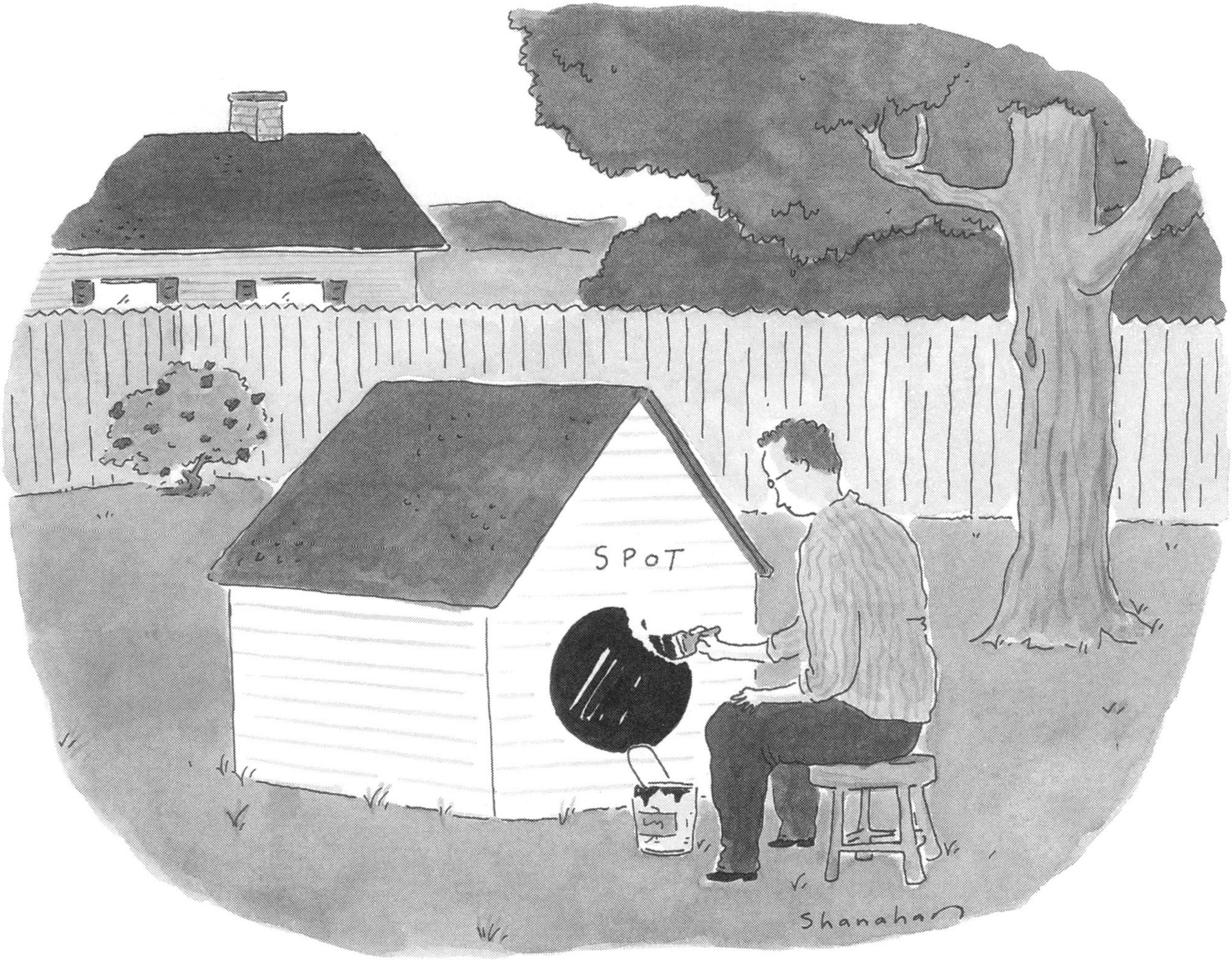
SPOT
Shanahan

"Now's your chance, Reuben. I've got her leveled off
at fifteen thousand feet, the weather is perfect, and we've
been cleared for landing. Why don't you take on over
and bring this baby down!"

THE PIE-EYED PIPER OF HAMELIN

83

"I understand your feelings, dear, but don't you think
that Jane Pauley would just as soon see you
keep your strength up?"

85

THE DEW DUNK INN

Hosts: Cheryl and Ted Wells

If you enjoy picture-postcard New England scenery, spectacular autumn foliage, and the lasting satisfaction of a monster dunk, give Cheryl and Ted a call! This restored Vermont farmhouse boasts a freshwater pond, acres of wooded riding trails, and eight pro-size indoor basketball courts! Ted's amazing repertoire of spin, double-pump, and alley-oop dunks is surpassed only by the myriad delights that spring from Cheryl's kitchen!

THE STAHL HOUSE

Hosts: Leigh and Andy Stahl

Situated on over 100 acres, this sprawling Georgia plantation house is the perfect place to get away from it all, Southern style. There's boating, biking, boccie, badminton, and, of course, basketball. Andy, a master of the trick dribble, will show even "all thumbs" guests how to beat the full-court press, run time off the clock, or just plain amaze their friends with their newly acquired ball-handling skills!

BLOCK ISLAND
BED-AND-BREAKFAST

Hosts: Nancy and Ed Ellis

Nancy and Ed are retired schoolteachers who have lovingly restored their 150-year-old house, turning it into an antique-laden paradise by the sea! During the warmer weather, breakfast is served on the attached oceanfront deck. Defensive specialists all of their lives, Nancy and Ed will not only shower you with hospitality, they'll also teach you the intricacies of the collapsing full-court press, the slap steal, the squeeze, the trap, shot blocking, or just getting in someone's face!

THE FAST BREAKERS

Hosts: Kay and Bernie Rasmussen

Located on the shores of picturesque East Bound Bay, this fairy-tale frame cottage will delight all comers. While Kay spoons up local color and local customs, Bernie will satisfy even the pickiest cager with generous servings of boxing out, crashing the boards, and hitting the outlet man on the fast break. Free time? Time for free throws with Kay, who during her high-school and collegiate career was a better than 90% shooter from the charity stripe!

Shanahan

"Nthng fr *Ls Msrbls* or *Phntm*. How bt *A Chrs Ln*?"

THE ADVENTURES OF WREN TIN TIN

"Do we have your blessing?"

"'What I Did on My Summer Vacation.'"

92

DISNEYWORLD, HO!
(AFTER WINSLOW HOMER)

THE EMBARRASSMENT OF EUROPA'S BOYFRIEND

"That ain't no ordinary footstool, Dusty. That there's
the king of the hassocks, all leather and a yard wide!
He's proud, powerful proud, but mark my words. Someday
soon someone'll catch him. He'll be roped, he'll be broke,
and he'll be rid. I'm aimin' to be that someone, Dusty!"